CRAZY FINGER SPINNER TRICKS

Awesome Skills, Tips & Hacks For Your Fidget Spinner

Created by Mickey MacIntyre

Contributors: Brodie Bell

Copyright © Bell & Mackenzie Publishing Limited 2017

ISBN: 978-1-912155-25-5

BELL & MACKENZIE
PUBLISHING LIMITED

www.bellmackenzie.com

CONTENTS

LEVEL 1: EASY   LEVEL 2: INTERMEDIATE   LEVEL 3: DIFFICULT

SINGLE HAND SPIN

* HOLD THE SPINNER IN ONE HAND USING YOUR THUMB AND INDEX FINGER ON THE TOP AND BOTTOM CENTRE CAPS SO THAT YOUR THUMB IS ON TOP AND YOUR FINGER UNDERNEATH.
* BRING YOUR MIDDLE FINGER BETWEEN TWO OF THE BEARING ARMS AND PRACTICE MOVING IT GENTLY BACK AND FORTH.
* WHEN YOU'RE READY, FLICK YOUR MIDDLE FINGER POWERFULLY UPWARDS TO PUT THE SPINNER IN MOTION.
* YOU CAN ALSO USE YOUR MIDDLE FINGER TO STOP THE SPINNER.

LEVEL 1

TABLE SPIN

* PLACE THE SPINNER ON A TABLE TOP USING THE INDEX FINGER OF ONE HAND ON THE CENTRE CAP TO HOLD IT IN PLACE THEN USE THE INDEX FINGER OF YOUR OTHER HAND TO GIVE IT A REALLY SHARP, STRONG FLICK. TAKE YOUR FINGER OFF.
* SEE HOW FAST YOU CAN SPIN IT AND HOW LONG YOU CAN KEEP IT ROTATING OFF A SINGLE FLICK. TWO MINUTES IS THE RECORD OUR END WHAT TIME CAN YOU GET?

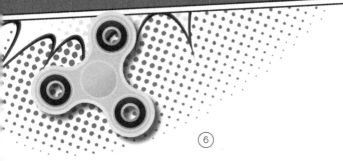

BOTTLE SPINNER

* FIND AN UNOPENED BOTTLE OF WATER OR JUICE AND PUT IT ON A FLAT SURFACE. PLACE THE SPINNER ON THE LID OF THE BOTTLE HOLDING IT IN PLACE WITH YOUR INDEX FINGER ON THE CENTRE CAP (TRY TO FIND A BOTTLE WHICH HAS A LID WITH A FLAT TOP).
* USE THE INDEX FINGER OF YOUR FREE HAND TO GIVE IT A SPIN THEN RELEASE THE FINGER HOLDING IT.
* SEE HOW LONG YOU CAN KEEP IT SPINNING ON THE BOTTLE BEFORE IT FALLS.

LEVEL 1

FINGER SPIN

* HOLD THE SPINNER IN ONE HAND USING YOUR THUMB AND INDEX FINGER ON THE TOP AND BOTTOM CENTRE CAPS (THUMB ON TOP) SO THAT THE SPINNER IS PARALLEL TO THE FLOOR AND IN A HORIZONTAL POSITION.
* GIVE IT A REALLY GOOD SPIN USING THE INDEX FINGER ON YOUR FREE HAND THEN RELEASE YOUR THUMB SO THAT THE SPINNER ROTATES FREELY BALANCED ON THE PAD OF YOUR FINGER. TRY BALANCING IT ON THE PAD OF YOUR THUMB TOO.

LEVEL 1

HAND DRYER SPIN

* IF YOU WANT TO GET YOUR SPINNER ROTATING AT CRAZY
  SPEEDS TRY THIS COOL TRICK.
* FIND AN ELECTRIC HAND DRYER (NOT A HAIR DRYER) THE
  KIND YOU WOULD SEE IN A PUBLIC TOILET/RESTROOM.
  IT NEEDS TO BE ONE OF THE MORE POWERFUL DRIERS.
* HOLD THE SPINNER IN ONE HAND USING YOUR THUMB
  AND INDEX FINGER ON THE CENTRE CAPS.
* HOLD IT UNDER THE HAND DRYER AND PRESS THE START
  BUTTON IF IT HAS ONE.
* WATCH THE SPINNER'S RPMs GO CRAZY.

LEVEL 1

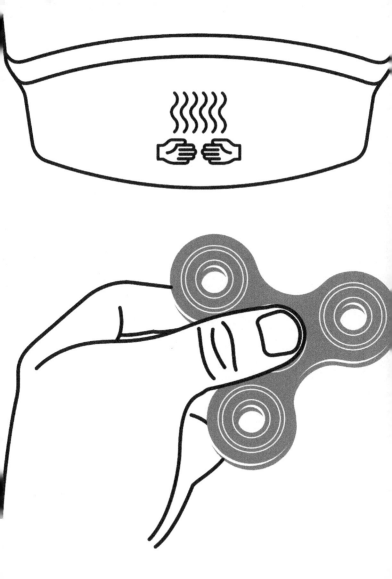

CHOPPERBLADES

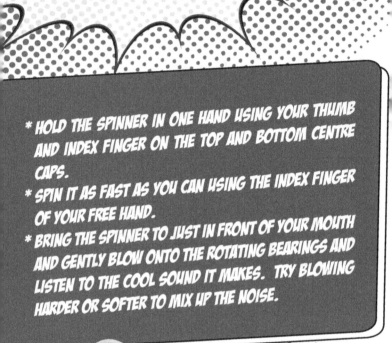

* HOLD THE SPINNER IN ONE HAND USING YOUR THUMB AND INDEX FINGER ON THE TOP AND BOTTOM CENTRE CAPS.
* SPIN IT AS FAST AS YOU CAN USING THE INDEX FINGER OF YOUR FREE HAND.
* BRING THE SPINNER TO JUST IN FRONT OF YOUR MOUTH AND GENTLY BLOW ONTO THE ROTATING BEARINGS AND LISTEN TO THE COOL SOUND IT MAKES. TRY BLOWING HARDER OR SOFTER TO MIX UP THE NOISE.

LEVEL 1

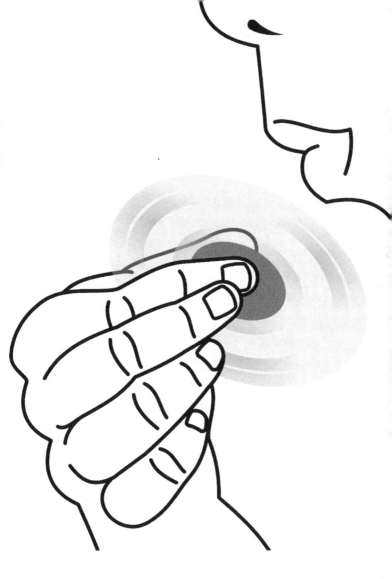

TABLE DROP

* SIT BY A TABLE OR FLAT SURFACE.
* HOLD THE SPINNER IN ONE HAND USING YOUR THUMB AND INDEX FINGER ON THE TOP AND BOTTOM CENTRE CAPS (THUMB ON TOP) SO THAT THE SPINNER IS PARALLEL TO THE TABLE AND IN A HORIZONTAL POSITION.
* GIVE IT A REALLY GOOD SPIN USING THE INDEX FINGER OF YOUR FREE HAND.
* TOSS THE SPINNER FORWARD AND DOWN ON TO THE TABLE RELEASING BOTH FINGERS AT THE SAME TIME AND TRYING TO KEEP THE SPINNER LEVEL.
* IF YOU GET IT RIGHT THE SPINNER SHOULD LAND EVENLY ON THE TABLE WHILE STILL ROTATING.

LEVEL 1

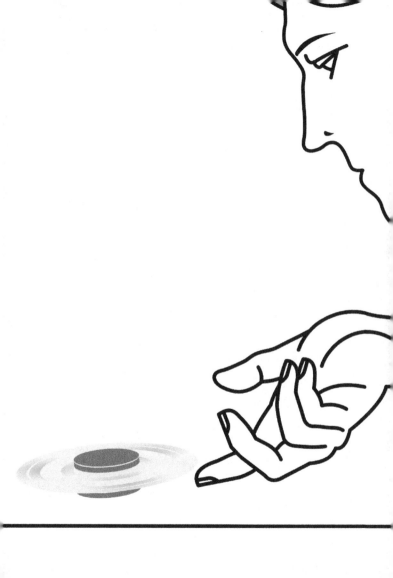

ROTATING HAND TO HAND

* HOLD THE SPINNER IN YOUR RIGHT HAND USING YOUR THUMB ON THE TOP CENTRE CAP AND YOUR YOUR INDEX AND MIDDLE FINGER ON THE BOTTOM CENTRE CAP.
* GIVE IT A REALLY GOOD SPIN USING THE INDEX FINGER OF YOUR LEFT HAND THEN RELEASE YOUR THUMB SO THAT THE SPINNER ROTATES FREELY BALANCED ON YOUR 2 FINGERS.
* WHILE THE SPINNER IS ROTATING PLACE THE INDEX AND MIDDLE FINGERS OF YOUR LEFT HAND ON THE TOP CENTRE CAP OF THE SPINNER THEN ROTATE BOTH HANDS 180 DEGREES SO THAT THE SPINNER IS NOW ON TOP OF THE FINGERS OF YOUR LEFT HAND.
* RELEASE THE FINGERS OF YOUR RIGHT HAND.
* PRACTICE PASSING FROM HAND TO HAND IN THIS MANNER WHILST KEEPING THE SPINNER ROTATING AT ALL TIMES.

DOUBLE CROSS

* YOU WILL NEED TWO SPINNERS FOR THIS TRICK.
* PLACE ONE SPINNER ON TOP OF THE OTHER SO THAT THE CENTRE CAPS MEET.
* HOLD THE SPINNERS BETWEEN YOUR THUMB AND INDEX FINGER.
* FIRSTLY GIVE ONE OF THEM A SPIN THEN SPIN THE OTHER IN THE OPPOSITE DIRECTION.
* THIS ONE LOOKS EVEN BETTER WHEN YOU HAVE TWO DIFFERENT COLOURED SPINNERS.

LEVEL 1

NOSE SPINNER

* SIT DOWN IN A CHAIR WITH THE SPINNER BALANCING ON THE HEEL OF YOUR HAND. HOLD IT IN PLACE WITH THE THUMB OF YOUR FREE HAND AND USE THE INDEX FINGER OF THE SAME HAND TO GET IT SPINNING.
* REMOVE YOUR THUMB AND BEND YOUR HEAD DOWN SO THAT THE TIP OF YOUR NOSE IS TOUCHING THE CENTRE CAP OF THE SPINNER.
* HOLDING THE SPINNER FIRMLY AGAINST YOUR NOSE TILT YOUR HEAD BACK AS FAR AS POSSIBLE SO YOU ARE LOOKING AT THE CEILING.
* WHEN YOU HAVE GOT THE ROTATING SPINNER STABLE ON YOUR NOSE TAKE THE HEEL OF YOUR HAND OFF THE SPINNER.
* WHEN YOU HAVE MASTERED THAT TRY STANDING UP WHEN YOU HAVE GOT THE SPINNER BALANCED.

LEVEL 2

POOL TABLE JUMP

* IF YOU HAVE A POOL OR SNOOKER TABLE THIS IS A COOL TRICK.
* PLACE THE BLACK BALL JUST IN FRONT OF AN OPEN POCKET ON THE POOL TABLE. LINE UP THE WHITE BALL APPROX. 15 INCHES AWAY FROM THE BLACK AT A 45 DEGREE ANGLE TO THE CUSHION AS IF YOU WERE SETTING THE BALLS UP TO POT THE BLACK.
* PLACE THE SPINNER IN BETWEEN THE TWO BALLS, HOLD IT IN PLACE WITH THE INDEX FINGER OF ONE HAND WHILE SPINNING WITH THE INDEX FINGER OF YOUR FREE HAND THEN LET GO OF THE SPINNER.
* TAKE A POOL CUE AND CHIP THE WHITE BALL OVER THE ROTATING SPINNER TO POT THE BLACK. IF YOU CAN PULL THIS TRICK OFF IT LOOKS SUPER COOL.

LEVEL 2

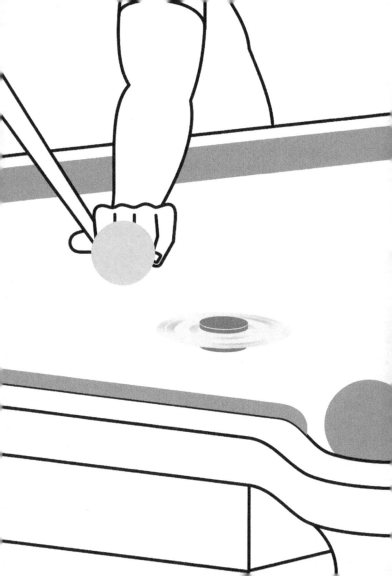

FLICK SPIN

* FIND YOURSELF A PENCIL.
* REMOVE BOTH OF THE CENTRE CAPS FROM THE SPINNER AND PLACE THE PENCIL THROUGH THE CENTRE HOLE SO THAT IT FITS TIGHT. (YOU MAY NEED TO ADD SOME STICKY TAPE TO THE PENCIL TO MAKE IT THICKER).
* THE TIP OF THE PENCIL SHOULD BE POINTING UPWARDS WITH THE SPINNER NEARER THE BOTTOM.
* HOLD THE PENCIL AND SPIN THE SPINNER WITH THE INDEX FINGER OF YOUR FREE HAND AND PLACE IT ON A TABLE.
* AS THE SPINNER AND PENCIL ROTATE, FLICK THE TIP OF THE PENCIL WITH YOUR FINGER. IF YOU HAVE IT SPINNING FAST ENOUGH WATCH HOW IT MOVES AROUND THE TABLE BUT DOESN'T TIP OVER NO MATTER HOW HARD YOU FLICK IT.

LEVEL 2

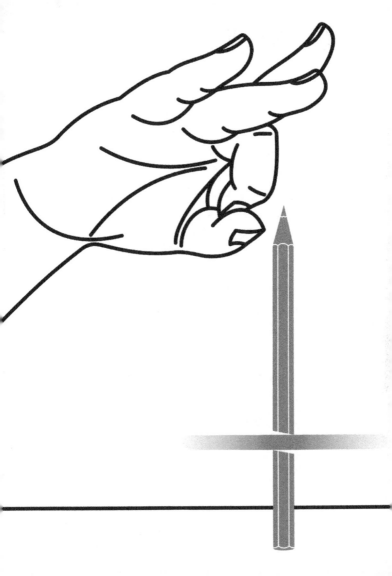

STRAIGHTENER

* FIND YOURSELF A PENCIL.
* REMOVE BOTH OF THE CENTRE CAPS FROM THE SPINNER AND PLACE THE PENCIL THROUGH THE CENTRE HOLE SO THAT IT IS TIGHT. (YOU MAY NEED TO ADD SOME STICKY TAPE TO THE PENCIL TO MAKE IT THICKER). THE TIP OF THE PENCIL SHOULD BE POINTING UPWARDS WITH THE SPINNER NEARER THE BOTTOM.
* HOLD THE PENCIL AND SPIN THE SPINNER WITH THE INDEX FINGER OF YOUR FREE HAND.
* PLACE THE SPINNING PENCIL AT A 45 DEGREE ANGLE ON A HARD SURFACE AND LET GO. THE SPINNER AND PENCIL WILL BE SPINNING SEEMINGLY OUT OF CONTROL BUT KEEP WATCHING. IN ABOUT 30 SECONDS THE PENCIL WILL COMPLETELY STRAIGHTEN UP IF YOU HAVE IT ROTATING FAST ENOUGH.

LEVEL 2

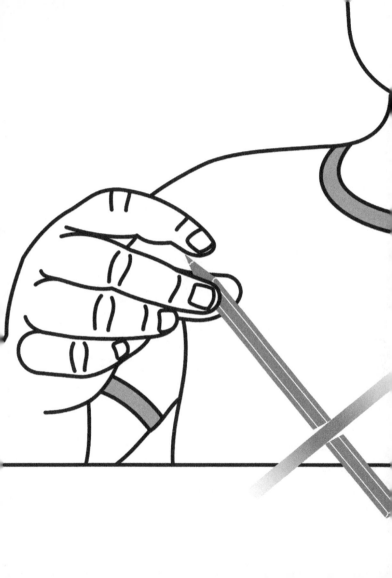

HAND TO HAND

* HOLD THE SPINNER IN ONE HAND USING YOUR THUMB AND INDEX FINGER ON THE TOP AND BOTTOM CENTRE CAPS (THUMB ON TOP).
* GIVE IT A REALLY GOOD SPIN USING THE INDEX FINGER OF YOUR FREE HAND THEN BEGIN SLOWLY PASSING THE SPINNER FROM HAND TO HAND WITH THUMB AND INDEX FINGER.
* WHEN PASSING PLACE YOUR FINGERS ON THE OUTER EDGE OF THE CENTRE CAP SO THE FINGERS ON THE ACCEPTING HAND HAVE ENOUGH ROOM TO HOLD IT.
* AS YOU GAIN CONFIDENCE, INCREASE THE SPEED THAT YOU PASS THE SPINNER.
* WHEN YOU'RE READY, TRY A SMALL TOSS FROM ONE HAND TO THE OTHER CONCENTRATING ON KEEPING THE SPINNER ROTATING THROUGHOUT THE TRICK.
* ONCE YOU HAVE MASTERED A SHORT TOSS START TO WIDEN THE GAP BETWEEN YOUR HANDS.
* WHEN YOU'RE REALLY GOOD TRY NOT LOOKING AT THE SPINNER AS YOU TOSS IT.

VERTICAL TOSS

* HOLD THE SPINNER IN ONE HAND USING YOUR THUMB AND INDEX FINGER ON THE CENTRE CAP. TURN THE SPINNER SO IT FACES YOUR BODY WITH YOUR THUMB CLOSEST TO YOUR BODY (SEE DIAGRAM).
* ROTATE THE SPINNER USING THE INDEX FINGER OF YOUR FREE HAND THEN TOSS FROM ONE HAND TO THE OTHER KEEPING IT VERTICAL AND ROTATING THROUGH THE TOSS AND THE CATCH.
* WHEN CATCHING TRY TO AIM JUST BELOW THE CENTRE CAP.

LEVEL 2

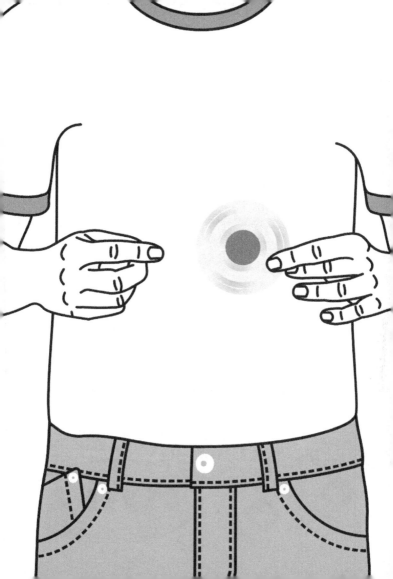

HAT TRICK

* HAVE A BASEBALL CAP TO HAND.
* PERFORM THE BASIC FINGER SPIN BY HOLDING THE SPINNER BETWEEN THE THUMB AND INDEX FINGER OF YOUR HAND (THUMB ON TOP).
* GIVE IT A SPIN USING THE INDEX FINGER OF YOUR FREE HAND THEN RELEASE THE THUMB FROM THE TOP CENTRE CAP SO THAT SPINNER BALANCES AND ROTATES FREELY ON YOUR FINGER.
* WITH YOUR FREE HAND PICK UP THE CAP BY THE PEAK AND SEE IF YOU CAN TOSS IT UP AND ON TO YOUR HEAD WHILST KEEPING THE SPINNER ROTATING AND BALANCED ON YOUR FINGER.

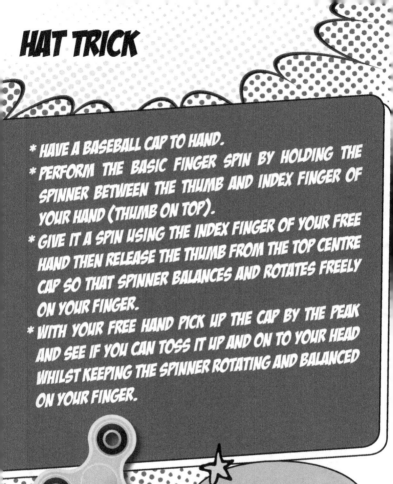

LEVEL 2

FINGER TIP SPIN

* SIMILAR TO THE BASIC FINGER SPIN - BUT INSTEAD OF IT BALANCING ON THE PAD OF YOUR INDEX FINGER, USE THE VERY TIP OF YOUR FINGER.
* HOLD THE SPINNER IN ONE HAND USING YOUR THUMB AND TIP OF YOUR INDEX FINGER ON THE TOP AND BOTTOM CENTRE CAPS (THUMB ON TOP) SO THAT THE SPINNER IS PARALLEL TO THE FLOOR AND IN A HORIZONTAL POSITION.
* GIVE IT A REALLY GOOD SPIN USING THE INDEX FINGER OF YOUR FREE HAND THEN RELEASE YOUR THUMB SO THAT THE SPINNER ROTATES FREELY BALANCED ON THE PAD OF YOUR FINGER. SLOWLY ALTER THE POSITION OF YOUR FINGER UNTIL THE SPINNER IS BALANCING ON THE TIP OF YOU FINGER.
* ONCE YOU HAVE LEARNED TO BALANCE THE SPINNER TRY GENTLY BENDING THE TIP OF YOUR FINGER AND TURNING YOUR FINGER A FRACTION TO THE LEFT THEN TO THE RIGHT TO CHANGE THE ORIENTATION AS IT SPINS.

STICK TRAP

* FIND A LONG ROD/STICK (IDEALLY WITH A FLAT TIP) THAT WHEN HELD IN YOUR OUTSTRETCHED ARM WILL REACH TO THE CEILING.
* HOLD THE SPINNER IN ONE HAND USING YOUR THUMB AND INDEX FINGER ON THE CENTRE CAPS.
* GIVE IT A REALLY GOOD SPIN USING THE INDEX FINGER OF YOUR FREE HAND. PICK UP THE ROD AND CAREFULLY TRANSFER THE SPINNER TO TIP OF THE ROD SO THAT IT BALANCES WHILST CONTINUING TO ROTATE.
* SLOWLY RAISE THE ROD TO THE CEILING AND TRAP THE SPINNER AGAINST THE CEILING UNTIL IT STOPS.

PENCIL BALANCE

* GRAB A PENCIL.
* HOLD THE SPINNER IN ONE HAND USING YOUR THUMB AND INDEX FINGER ON THE CENTRE.
* GIVE IT A REALLY GOOD SPIN USING THE INDEX FINGER OF YOUR FREE HAND. PICK UP THE PENCIL AND TRANSFER THE ROTATING SPINNER ONTO THE TIP ON THE PENCIL. LET GO OF THE SPINNER WITH YOUR HAND AND BALANCE THE SPINNER ON THE PENCIL TIP.
* THIS IS REALLY TRICKY. YOU MIGHT FIND IT EASIER USING A CHOPSTICK WHICH HAS A BLUNT END.

LEVEL 2

BOTTLE BALANCE

* GRAB A PENCIL.
* REMOVE BOTH OF THE CENTRE CAPS FROM THE SPINNER AND PLACE THE PEN OR PENCIL THROUGH THE CENTRE HOLE SO THAT IT IS A TIGHT FIT (YOU MAY NEED TO ADD SOME STICKY TAPE TO THE PENCIL TO MAKE IT THICKER).
* THE TIP OF THE PENCIL SHOULD BE POINTING DOWNWARDS WITH THE SPINNER NEARER THE BOTTOM.
* HOLD THE PENCIL UPRIGHT USING THE INDEX FINGER OF ONE HAND WITH THE TIP ON A HARD FLAT SURFACE AND SPIN THE SPINNER WITH THE INDEX FINGER OF YOUR FREE HAND.
* HOLD THE SPINNER IN ONE HAND USING YOUR THUMB AND INDEX FINGER ON THE CENTRE
* RELEASE THE INDEX FINGER HOLDING THE PEN OR PENCIL AND WATCH IT SPIN.
* WHEN YOU'RE GOOD AT THIS, FIND A WATER BOTTLE (MAKE SURE THERE IS WATER INSIDE TO STABILISE THE BOTTLE) AND REPEAT THE ABOVE INSTRUCTIONS THIS TIME BALANCING THE TIP OF THE PEN OR PENCIL ON THE LID OF THE BOTTLE.
* YOU'LL BE AMAZED AT THE CRAZY ANGLES IT TURNS AT.

STRING SPINNER

* USING THE SAME PENCIL WITH SPINNER ATTACHED FROM THE PREVIOUS PAGE. TIE A LENGTH OF STRING FIRMLY TO THE SHORTEST END OF THE PENCIL TIGHT AGAINST THE SPINNER.
* HOLDING THE PENCIL IN ONE HAND GIVE THE SPINNER A SPIN WITH YOUR FREE HAND THEN HOLD THE END OF THE STRING AND WATCH HOW IT DOUBLE ROTATES. SUPER COOL.

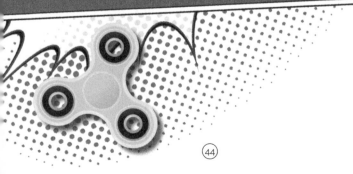

LEVEL 2

QUAD TOWER

* THIS IS A SIMILAR TRICK TO DOUBLE CROSS BUT WITH FOUR SPINNERS SO YOU MIGHT NEED TO JOIN FORCES WITH YOUR FRIENDS TO GET ENOUGH SPINNERS.
* LINE UP 4 SPINNERS (DIFFERENT COLOURS IF YOU HAVE THEM) ON TOP OF EACH OTHER SO THAT THE CENTRE CAPS MEET.
* HOLD THE SPINNERS BETWEEN YOUR THUMB AND INDEX FINGER OR BETWEEN YOUR THUMB AND MIDDLE FINGER IF THAT'S EASIER.
* GIVE EACH A SPIN IN TURN, TRYING DIFFERENT DIRECTIONS SO THEY ARE ALL SPINNING SIMULTANEOUSLY.

LEVEL 2

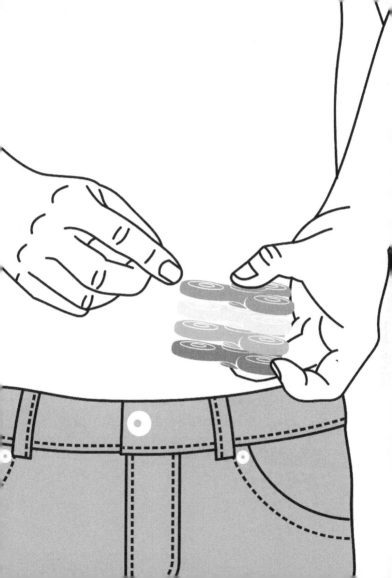

FINGER TO FINGER

* HOLD THE SPINNER IN ONE HAND USING YOUR THUMB AND INDEX FINGER ON THE CENTRE CAPS (THUMB ON TOP/KNUCKLES POINTING DOWN TO THE FLOOR).
* GIVE IT A REALLY GOOD SPIN USING THE INDEX FINGER OF YOUR FREE HAND.
* WHILE ALWAYS KEEPING TWO FINGERS ON THE SPINNER BRING YOUR MIDDLE FINGER TO THE UNDERSIDE CENTRE CAP WHILE SIMULTANEOUSLY REMOVING YOUR INDEX FINGER.
* REVERSE THIS PROCESS BY BRINGING YOUR INDEX FINGER BACK TO THE UNDERSIDE CENTRE CAP WHILE REMOVING YOUR MIDDLE FINGER.
* WHEN YOU HAVE MASTERED THIS MOVE PRACTICE MOVING TO DIFFERENT FINGERS ON YOUR HAND.

LEVEL 2

REVERSE FLIP

* HOLD THE SPINNER BY ONE OF ITS ARMS (NOT THE CENTRE) USING YOUR THUMB AND TWO FINGERS. MAKE SURE THE SPINNER FACES YOUR BODY WITH YOUR THUMB CLOSEST TO YOU.
* FLICK THE SPINNER UP BY ITS ARM AND CATCH IT IN THE CENTRE IN A PINCH GRIP AS IT ROTATES.
* YOU DON'T NEED TO FLICK IT HIGH AT ALL. IT'S ALMOST LIKE A MAGIC TRICK/SLEIGHT OF HAND WHERE YOU START THE SPIN WITH ONE GRIP AND FINISH WITH ANOTHER.

LEVEL 2

HOT POTATO FINGERTIPS

* HOLD THE SPINNER IN ONE HAND USING YOUR THUMB AND INDEX FINGER ON THE TOP AND BOTTOM CENTRE CAPS (THUMB ON TOP) SO THAT THE SPINNER IS PARALLEL TO THE FLOOR AND IN A HORIZONTAL POSITION.
* GIVE IT A REALLY GOOD SPIN USING THE INDEX FINGER OF YOUR FREE HAND THEN RELEASE YOUR THUMB SO THAT THE SPINNER ROTATES FREELY BALANCED ON YOUR FINGER.
* CAREFULLY BUT FORCEFULLY TOSS THE SPINNER UPWARDS OFF YOUR INDEX FINGER AND ONTO YOUR MIDDLE FINGER KEEPING THE SPINNER IN A HORIZONTAL POSITION AND ROTATING THROUGHOUT. REPEAT THE MOVEMENT TO YOUR THIRD FINGER, PINKIE AND THEN BACK AGAIN UNTIL YOU REACH YOUR INDEX FINGER.
* YOU SHOULD ONLY TOSS THE SPINNER 1 OR 2 INCHES HIGH EACH TIME KEEPING IT CONSTANTLY ROTATING. THIS WILL TAKE A LOT OF PRACTICE BUT WILL AMAZE YOUR FRIENDS ONCE YOU'VE MASTERED IT.

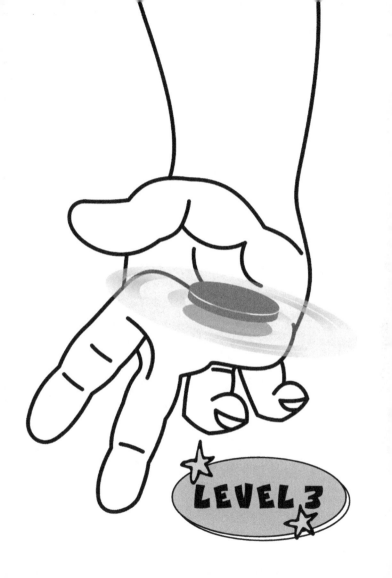

LEVEL 3

KNUCKLE CATCH

* HOLD THE SPINNER IN ONE HAND USING YOUR THUMB AND INDEX FINGER ON THE TOP AND BOTTOM CENTRE CAPS (THUMB ON TOP) SO THAT THE SPINNER IS PARALLEL TO THE FLOOR AND IN A HORIZONTAL POSITION.
* GIVE IT A REALLY GOOD SPIN USING THE INDEX FINGER OF YOUR FREE HAND THEN RELEASE YOUR THUMB SO THAT THE SPINNER ROTATES FREELY BALANCED ON YOUR FINGER.
* CAREFULLY BUT FORCEFULLY TOSS THE SPINNER UPWARDS OFF YOUR INDEX FINGER THEN QUICKLY TURN YOUR HAND AROUND SO THAT YOUR PALM IS FACING DOWNWARDS.
* BEND YOUR INDEX FINGER AND HAVE IT RAISED HIGHER THAN THE OTHER FINGERS ON YOUR HAND AND CATCH THE SPINNER SO THAT IT LANDS ON THE KNUCKLE OF YOUR INDEX FINGER.
* THE FLICK OF YOUR HAND AND POSITIONING OF YOUR KNUCKLE NEEDS TO BE VERY FAST & ACCURATE TO KEEP THE SPINNER ROTATING CONSTANTLY.
* ONCE YOU HAVE MASTERED IT REVERSE THE MOVEMENT SO THAT THE SPINNER IS TOSSED FROM YOUR KNUCKLE BACK ON TO YOUR INDEX FINGER OR MIDDLE FINGER.

KNUCKLE TAP

* THIS IS A VARIATION OF THE KNUCKLE CATCH TRICK SO MASTER THAT FIRST BEFORE MOVING ON TO THIS TRICK.
* HOLD THE SPINNER IN ONE HAND USING YOUR THUMB AND INDEX FINGER ON THE TOP AND BOTTOM CENTRE CAPS SO THAT THE SPINNER IS PARALLEL TO THE FLOOR AND IN A HORIZONTAL POSITION.
* GIVE IT A REALLY GOOD SPIN USING THE INDEX FINGER OF YOUR FREE HAND THEN RELEASE YOUR THUMB SO THAT THE SPINNER ROTATES FREELY BALANCED ON YOUR FINGER.
* TOSS THE SPINNER UPWARDS OFF YOUR INDEX FINGER THEN QUICKLY TURN YOUR HAND AROUND SO THAT YOUR PALM IS FACING DOWNWARDS.
* BEND YOUR INDEX FINGER AND HAVE IT RAISED HIGHER THAN THE OTHER FINGERS ON YOUR HAND AND CATCH THE SPINNER SO THAT IT LANDS ON YOUR KNUCKLE.
* REVERSE THE MOVEMENT SO THAT THE SPINNER IS TOSSED FROM YOUR KNUCKLE BACK ON TO YOUR MIDDLE FINGER.
* IMMEDIATELY TOSS AGAIN BUT HAVE THE SPINNER LAND ON THE KNUCKLE OF YOUR MIDDLE FINGER.
* REVERSE THE MOVEMENT SO THAT THE SPINNER IS TOSSED FROM YOUR KNUCKLE BACK ON TO YOUR INDEX FINGER.

UNDER ARM THROW

* HOLD THE SPINNER IN YOUR LEFT HAND USING YOUR THUMB AND INDEX FINGER ON THE CENTRE CAPS (THUMB ON TOP) IN A REGULAR PINCH GRIP. MAKE SURE THE SPINNER FACES YOUR BODY WITH YOUR THUMB CLOSEST TO YOU.
* GIVE IT A REALLY GOOD SPIN USING THE INDEX FINGER OF YOUR FREE HAND.
* MOVE THE HAND WITH THE SPINNER UNDERNEATH YOUR RIGHT HAND SO THAT YOUR ARMS ARE MOMENTARILY CROSSED AT CHEST HEIGHT. THROW THE SPINNER GENTLY UP TO THE HEIGHT OF YOUR EYE-LINE. UNCROSS YOUR ARMS AND CATCH THE FLYING SPINNER WITH A PINCH GRIP IN YOUR RIGHT HAND.
* THIS ALL NEEDS TO BE DONE WITH ONE SMOOTH MOVEMENT WITH THE SPINNER ROTATING CONSTANTLY.

UNDER ARM COMBO

* HOLD THE SPINNER IN YOUR LEFT HAND USING YOUR THUMB AND INDEX FINGER ON THE CENTRE CAPS (THUMB ON TOP) IN A REGULAR PINCH GRIP. MAKE SURE THE SPINNER FACES YOUR BODY WITH YOUR THUMB CLOSEST TO YOU.
* GIVE IT A REALLY GOOD SPIN USING THE INDEX FINGER OF YOUR FREE HAND.
* MOVE THE HAND WITH THE SPINNER UNDERNEATH YOUR RIGHT HAND SO THAT YOUR ARMS ARE MOMENTARILY CROSSED AT CHEST HEIGHT. THROW THE SPINNER GENTLY UP TO THE HEIGHT OF YOUR EYE-LINE. UNCROSS YOUR ARMS AND CATCH THE FLYING SPINNER WITH A PINCH GRIP IN YOUR RIGHT HAND.
* HOLD IT FOR JUST A SECOND POSITIONED VERTICALLY TO YOUR BODY BEFORE TOSSING ACROSS TO THE OTHER HAND FOR THE SWITCH.
* THIS ALL NEEDS TO BE DONE IN TWO SMOOTH MOVEMENTS WITH THE SPINNER ROTATING CONSTANTLY.
* THIS KILLER COMBO OF COMPLEXITY COULD BLOW YOUR MIND BUT DON'T THINK YOU'VE MASTERED THE SPINNER, IT'S NOT EVEN THE HARDEST TRICK IN THE BOOK. THAT COMES NEXT...

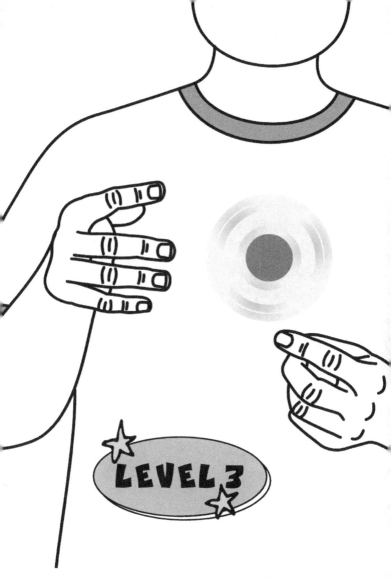

OVER THE TOP

* WHAT YOU ARE TRYING TO DO HERE IS THROW THE SPINNER UP FROM BEHIND YOUR BACK AND OVER YOUR SHOULDER TO CATCH IT IN FRONT OF YOU.

* HOLD THE SPINNER IN YOUR LEFT HAND WITH YOUR THUMB AND INDEX FINGER ON THE CENTRE CAPS (THUMB ON TOP) MAKING SURE THE SPINNER FACES YOUR BODY WITH YOUR THUMB CLOSEST TO YOUR CHEST. GET IT SPINNING AS USUAL, GOOD AND FAST. BRING YOUR LEFT HAND BEHIND YOUR BACK WITH THE ELBOW POINTING TO THE FLOOR (AS IF YOU WERE TRYING TO ITCH YOUR BACK). TOSS THE SPINNER UP AND OVER YOUR RIGHT SHOULDER IN FRONT OF YOUR BODY AND CATCH IT IN A PINCH GRIP IN FRONT OF YOU WITH YOUR RIGHT HAND WHILST IT'S STILL SPINNING.

* SUPER DIFFICULT. THIS TRICK CAN LITERALLY TAKE YOU WEEKS TO MASTER AND IS THE HARDEST TRICK IN THE BOOK.

TRICK	COMPLETED ✔	TIME COMPLETED	
		HRS	MIN
SINGLE HAND SPIN			
TABLE SPIN			
BOTTLE SPINNER			
FINGER SPIN			
HAND DRYER SPIN			
CHOPPERBLADES			
TABLE DROP			
ROTATING HAND TO HAND			
DOUBLE CROSS			
NOSE SPINNER			
POOL TABLE JUMP			
FLICK SPIN			
STRAIGHTENER			
HAND TO HAND			
VERTICAL TOSS			
HAT TRICK			
FINGER TIP SPIN			
STICK TRAP			
PENCIL BALANCE			
BOTTLE BALANCE			
STRING SPINNER			
QUAD TOWER			
FINGER TO FINGER			
REVERSE FLIP			
HOT POTATO FINGERTIPS			
KNUCKLE CATCH			
KNUCKLE TAP			
UNDER ARM THROW			
UNDER ARM COMBO			
OVER THE TOP			

Made in the USA
Middletown, DE
04 November 2018